NOWHERE FAR FROM THE SEA

The story of New Zealand in Quotations

A catalogue record for this book is available from the National Library of New Zealand

ISBN 978-1-77694-025-7

A White Cloud Book
Published in 2023 by Upstart Press Ltd.
26 Greenpark Road, Penrose, Auckland 1061
New Zealand

www.upstartpress.co.nz

Quotations as sourced. Compiled by Stephen Barnett
Design and Format © Upstart Press 2023
The moral rights of the author have been asserted.

Design by www.cvdgraphics.co.nz

Printed in China by 1010 Printing

ACKNOWLEDGEMENTS

All efforts were made to secure approval for quotations where this was required. While it wasn't possible to contact all such copyright holders, acknowledgement has been made, as it has for all of the quotations appearing. My thanks to those who gave their permission. For permission to use text material appearing in the biographical notes, the compiler wishes to acknowledge the Ministry for Culture and Heritage, and Wikipedia.

INTRODUCTION

What it is about New Zealand and New Zealanders that impresses itself so on those who live here and on visitors to the country. Because, there is a special something about the place and its people that both appeals and intrigues.

The quotations gathered here form an arc in time from past to present, quotations from those who found their way here and settled, from explorers and visitors to this country, from writers and poets, artists, politicians and humorists, conservationists and more. From their words can be garnered at least part of the answer, in the sum of such as the country's geographical situation (far-flung, remote), its landscape (magnificent), natural environment (unique), its people (practical, of an innate goodness), the space and the solitude. Also, New Zealand is still a young country, still somewhat unshaped, and perhaps that too is part of the equation.

Stephen Barnett

"Whatungarongaro te tangata, toitū te whenua
People come and go but the land remains.

— *Maori proverb*

Abel Janszoon Tasman (1603–1659) was a Dutch seafarer, explorer, and merchant, best known for his voyages of 1642 and 1644 in the service of the Dutch East India Company. Together with Franchoijs Jacobszoon Visscher, the two-ship expedition left from Batavia in August 1642 and in November, reached the west coast of Tasmania. Steering east, on 13 December 1642 they made what was the first recorded sighting of New Zealand, the north-west coast of the South Island – his 'great land uplifted high'.

Towards the middle of the day we saw a great land uplifted high. We had it S.E. of us, about 60 miles away.

— *Abel Janszoon Tasman (on the first recorded European sighting of New Zealand – of the Southern Alps; from Tasman's log)*

Sydney Parkinson (c.1745 –1771) was a Scottish botanical illustrator and natural history artist. He was the first European artist to visit Australia, New Zealand and Tahiti. Parkinson was employed by Joseph Banks to travel with him on James Cook's first voyage to the Pacific in 1768, on HMS *Endeavour*. Parkinson made nearly a thousand drawings of plants and animals collected by Banks and Daniel Solander on the voyage. He had to work in difficult conditions, living and working in a small cabin surrounded by hundreds of specimens.

On the 16th, having a breeze, we sailed along the shore of the land we had passed the day before, which appeared as wild and romantic as can be conceived. Rocks and mountains, whose tops were covered with snow, rose in view one above another from the water's edge: and those near the shore were clothed with wood, as well as some of the valleys between the hills, whose summits reached the clouds.

— *Sydney Parkinson (first impressions of New Zealand -* The Journals of Captain James Cook, *Beaglehole, J. C. (ed.), The Hakluyt Society, 1955)*

Ivan Mikhailovich Simonov (1794–1855) was a Russian astronomer and geodesist. After completing his studies he became a professor of physics at Kazan State University where he was a close friend of mathematician Nikolai Lobachevsky. He later went on to become the rector of Kazan State University. From 1819 to 1821 he took part in and wrote a detailed account of F. F. Bellingshausen and M. P. Lazarev's expedition around the world, during which the continent of Antarctica was discovered and also, in 1820, visited for a few days the Marlborough Sounds.

" . . . my ear was struck by the most delightful blending of the sounds of birdsong . . . nor do I recall having hear such a harmonious choir of songbirds anywhere in the remaining five parts of the earth; . . . "

— *Ivan Mikhailovich Simonov*

Arthur Saunders Thomson (1816–1860) was a notable New Zealand military surgeon, medical scientist, writer and historian. Born in Arbroath, Angus, Scotland, he joined the British Army in 1838 as an assistant surgeon and was stationed in India until 1847. There, he wrote about the epidemic of fever among his regiment during the monsoon season. Upon his return to England, he was appointed surgeon to the 58th Regiment of Foot and sent to New Zealand. In New Zealand he wrote extensively about disease statistics among Māori and European populations and about climatology.

New Zealand has been rendered famous by its climate . . . it has been styled delightful and pleasant, terms which convey the idea of an atmosphere rarely disturbed by wind and rain, whereas there are few countries on the globe where wind and rain are so frequent and so uncertain.

— *Dr Arthur Saunders Thomson,*
(The Story of New Zealand, *J. Murray, 1859*)

Sarah Amelia Courage (1845?-1901) was born in England, later emigrating to New Zealand with her husband and daughter, arriving in Lyttelton in 1864. The family farmed at Double Corner Station (also known as Waipara Station) near Leithfield, and later Seadown Station, near Amberley, both in North Canterbury. In 1896 she had published her satirical reminiscences *Lights and Shadows of Colonial Life*. Courage returned to England in 1899.

People from town are always impressed with the stillness of the country, a peaceful harmonious stillness, soothed by sweet smells and sweeter sounds – the bellbird's note, a note equal in rich melody to the blackbird of thrush in England; the murmur of the sea . . . and the sizzling noise the locusts or cicadas are making in the tussock.

— *Sarah Amelia Courage (*Lights and Shadows of Colonial Life*, private publication, 1896)*

Mary Anne Barker, Lady Barker (1831–1911) was an English author. Following the death of her first husband, Barker married Frederick Napier Broome and later sailed for New Zealand where they took up residence at the sheep station Steventon. After returning to London, Mary Anne Broome - still calling herself 'Lady Barker' - became a correspondent for *The Times* and published two books of verse. In 1870, she published *Station Life in New Zealand*, a collection of her letters home. Over the next eight years, Lady Barker wrote ten more books, including a sequel to *Station Life* entitled *Station Amusements in New Zealand*.

"We have a great deal of disagreeable weather, and a small proportion of bad weather, but in no other part of the world, I believe, does Nature so thoroughly understand how to make a fine day as in New Zealand.

— Lady Mary Anne Barker

Mark Twain, the pen name of **Samuel Langhorne Clemens** (1835–1910), was an American writer, humorist, entrepreneur, publisher, and lecturer. His novels include *The Adventures of Tom Sawyer* and its sequel, *Adventures of Huckleberry Finn*. Twain was raised in Hannibal, Missouri, which later provided the setting for *Tom Sawyer* and *Huckleberry Finn*. He served an apprenticeship with a printer and then later became a riverboat pilot on the Mississippi River. His wit and satire, in prose and in speech, earned praise from critics and peers, and he was a friend to presidents, artists, industrialists, and European royalty.

> If it would not look too much like showing off, I would tell the reader where New Zealand is.

— *Mark Twain* (Following the Equator, American Publishing Co., 1899

> They stopped here on their way from home to heaven – thinking they had arrived.

— *Mark Twain (on Dunedin)*

Richard Treacy Henry (1845–1929) was a New Zealand conservationist who became an expert on the natural history of the country's flightless birds, especially the kākāpō. Born in Ireland, his family migrated to Australia in 1851. Henry moved to New Zealand in the 1870s, settling at Lake Te Anau in 1883 where he worked as a handyman, rabbiter, shepherd, taxidermist, boat-builder, explorer and guide, while studying the region's birdlife. Concern at the time that introduced mustelids were having a devastating effect on birdlife led to Resolution Island in Fiordland becoming a reserve and in 1894 Henry was appointed its curator and caretaker.

"This is fine country for the waterproof explorer.

— *Richard Henry (on New Zealand's Fiordland region)*

William Pember Reeves (1857–1932) was a New Zealand politician, cricketer, historian and poet who promoted social reform. Before entering politics, Reeves was a lawyer and journalist. During the premierships of John Ballance (1891–93) and Richard Seddon (1893–1906) he served as Minister of Labour, Minister of Education, Minister of Justice, and Commissioner of Stamp Duties. In 1896 Reeves left New Zealand for London, where he became Director of the London School of Economics (1908–19). Reeves's more influential writings include his history of New Zealand, *The Long White Cloud* (1898) and *State Experiments in Australia and New Zealand* (1902).

"The first European to find New Zealand was a Dutch sea-captain who was looking for something else. It takes its name from a province of Holland to which it does not bear the remotest likeness, and is usually regarded as the antipodes of England, but is not. Taken possession of by an English navigator, whose action was afterwards reversed by his country's rulers, it was only annexed by the English Government which did not want it, to keep it from the French who did.

— *William Pember Reeves*

Charles Blomfield (1848–1926) was an English-born artist famous for his paintings of New Zealand landscapes. Following the death of his father, Blomfield's mother brought her family to New Zealand, arriving in February 1863. As well as an exhibiting easel painter, Blomfield worked as a sign-writer and interior decorator. He travelled throughout the centre of the North Island on several occasions in the 1870s and 1880s creating many landscape paintings of the New Zealand countryside including the Pink and White Terraces, later destroyed in the 1886 eruption of Mt Tarawera.

I have never ceased to be thankful for two things. One is that I was born with an intense love for the beauty of Nature, and the other that I came to New Zealand before the hand of man had spoiled most of its natural beauty.

— *Charles Blomfield*

André Siegfried (1875–1959) was a French academic, geographer and political writer best known to English speakers for his commentaries on American, Canadian, and British politics.

". . . the first impression which one receives is of these two 'little islands of New Zealand lost in the immensity of the Ocean'. But they are little only because of the almost fearful solitude which surrounds them.

— *André Siegfried* (Democracy in New Zealand, *G. Bell & Sons, 1914*)

Sir Arthur Ignatius Conan Doyle (1859–1930) was a British writer and physician. He created the character Sherlock Holmes in 1887 for *A Study in Scarlet*, the first of four novels and fifty-six short stories about Holmes and Dr Watson. Doyle was a prolific writer; other than Holmes stories, his works include fantasy and science fiction stories, and humorous stories as well as plays, romances, poetry, non-fiction, and historical novels. In 1920, Doyle travelled to Australia and New Zealand on spiritualist missionary work, and over the next several years, until his death, he continued this mission in Britain, Europe, and the United States.

Farewell, New Zealand! I shall never see you again, but perhaps some memory of my visit may remain . . . Every man looks on his own country as God's own country if it be a free land, but the New Zealander has more reason than most . . .

— *Sir Arthur Conan Doyle*

Arnold Wall (1869–1966) was a New Zealand university professor, philologist, poet, mountaineer, botanist, writer and radio broadcaster. Born in Ceylon (Sri Lanka), he was educated at Harrow and Christ's College, Cambridge. Later, in 1898, Wall applied successfully for the chair of English language, literature and history at Canterbury College in New Zealand. Aside from his academic and literary pursuits, Wall had a love of outdoor activities and an intense interest in nature. Mountaineering expeditions in the Southern Alps led to a specialist interest in botany. In the 1920s he became honorary keeper of the herbarium in the Canterbury Museum.

Each of her streets is closed with shining Alps,
Like Heaven at the end of long plain lives.

– *Arnold Wall (on Christchurch: 'The City from the Hills',*
Alexander, W. F. and Currie, A. E. (compilers), A Treasury
of New Zealand Verse, *Whitcombe & Tombs, 1926)*

Kathleen Mansfield Murry (1888–1923) was a New Zealand writer, essayist and journalist, widely considered one of the most influential and important authors of the modernist movement. Her works are celebrated across the world. Mansfield wrote short stories and poetry which explored anxiety, sexuality and existentialism alongside a developing New Zealand identity. When she was 19, she left New Zealand and settled in England, where she became a friend of D. H. Lawrence, Virginia Woolf, Lady Ottoline Morrell and others in the orbit of the Bloomsbury Group. Mansfield was diagnosed with pulmonary tuberculosis in 1917, and she died in France aged 34.

". . . and always my thoughts go back to New Zealand — rediscovering it, finding beauty in it, re-living it.

— *Katherine Mansfield* (The Letters of Katherine Mansfield, *Constable, 1928*)

"It was an exquisite day. It was one of those days so clear, so still, so silent, you almost feel the earth itself has stopped in astonishment at its own beauty.

— Katherine Mansfield (on the Marlborough Sounds: 'Down the Sounds', Journal of Katherine Mansfield, Murry, John Middleton (ed.), Constable, 1954)

The more I see of life, the more certain I feel that it's the people who live remote from cities who inherit the earth. . . . And another thing is the longer I live the more I turn to New Zealand. I thank God I was born in New Zealand. A young country is a real heritage, though it takes some time to recognise it. But New Zealand is in my very bones.

— *Katherine Mansfield (*The Letters of Katherine Mansfield, *Constable, 1928)*

Robin Hyde, the pseudonym used by **Iris Guiver Wilkinson** (1906–1939), was a South African-born New Zealand poet, journalist and novelist. After schooling at Wellington Girls' College she briefly attended Victoria University. In 1925 she became a journalist for Wellington's *Dominion* newspaper, mostly writing for the women's pages. She continued to support herself through journalism throughout her life. In 1929 Hyde published her first book of poetry, *The Desolate Star*. Between 1935 and 1938 she published five novels: *Passport to Hell, Check To Your King, Wednesday's Children, Nor the Years Condemn* and *The Godwits Fly*.

". . . most of us here are human godwits; our north is mostly England. Our youth, our best, our intelligent, brave and beautiful, must make the long migration, under a compulsion they hardly understand; or else be dissatisfied all their lives long. They are the godwits.

— *Robin Hyde* (The Godwits Fly, *Hurst & Blackett, 1938*)

"Remember us for this, if for nothing else: in our generation, and of our own initiative, we loved England still, but we ceased to be 'for ever England'. We became, for as long as we have a country, New Zealand.

-Robin Hyde (T'ien Hsia Monthly, Shanghai, 1938)

George Bernard Shaw (1856–1950) was an Irish playwright, critic, polemicist and political activist. His influence on Western theatre, culture and politics extended from the 1880s to his death and beyond. He wrote more than sixty plays, including major works such as *Man and Superman* (1902), *Pygmalion* (1913) and *Saint Joan* (1923). With a range incorporating both contemporary satire and historical allegory, Shaw became the leading dramatist of his generation, and in 1925 was awarded the Nobel Prize in Literature. His reputation and fame were global and when in 1934 Shaw visited New Zealand, the country was captivated.

If I showed my true feelings I would cry; it's the best country I have been in.

— *George Bernard Shaw (*What I Said in New Zealand, *The Commercial Printing Co. of New Zealand, 1934)*

Altogether too many sheep.

— *George Bernard Shaw (reportedly in reply to a reporter in 1934 when asked for his impression of the country)*

"The trouble with New Zealand is that it is rather too pleasing a place. There is a danger of it being over-run by the riff raff of Europe. I suggest it might be a good idea to instruct the Tourist Department to say something about the horrors of New Zealand.

— *George Bernard Shaw (reported in the* Evening Post, *Wellington, 14 April 1934)*

Te Puea Hērangi (1883–1952), known by the name **Princess Te Puea**, was a Māori leader from the Waikato region. Her mother, Tiahuia, was the elder sister of King Mahuta. In her twenties, Te Puea settled at Mangatāwhiri and began dairy farming. She began collecting and recording waiata, whakapapa and and kōrero tawhito from her extended family.

"The land is our mother and father. It is the loving parent who nourishes us, sustains us . . . When we die it folds us in its arms

Princess Hērangi Te Puea (1939, quoted by Michael King in Te Puea 1978)

John Alan Edward Mulgan (1911–1945) was a New Zealand writer, journalist and editor, and the elder son of journalist and writer Alan Mulgan. He is best known for his novel *Man Alone* (1939). Mulgan studied at Auckland University College before attending Merton College in Oxford from 1933. With war on the horizon he joined the Territorial Army in 1938. Posted to the Middle East in 1942, Mulgan was promoted to major and made second-in-command of his regiment. In 1943 he was sent to Greece to coordinate guerilla action against the German forces. He was awarded the Military Cross for his actions.

" . . . New Zealanders are often wanderers and restless . . . They come from the most beautiful country in the world, but it is a small country and very remote. After a while this isolation oppresses then and they go abroad. They roam the world looking not for adventure but for satisfaction. . . . They are a queer, lost eccentric, pervading people who will seldom admit to the deep desire that is in all of them to go home and live quietly in New Zealand again.

— *John Mulgan* (Report on Experience, *Oxford University Press, 1947*)

John Boynton Priestley (1894–1984) was an English novelist, playwright, screenwriter, broadcaster and social commentator. His novel *The Good Companions* (1929) brought him to wide public notice. Many of his plays are structured around a time slip, and he went on to develop a new theory of time, with different dimensions that link past, present and future. In 1940 he broadcast a series of short propaganda radio talks, which were credited with strengthening civilian morale during the Battle of Britain. In the following years his left-wing beliefs brought him into conflict with the government and influenced the development of the welfare state.

"Watching this daily show of efficiency made me wonder if this easy New Zealand manner, the hearty shirt-sleeves-and-shorts style, didn't mask quite a talent for organisation. They look and sound these chaps, as if they could hardly bother to keep the country running but then you find they are running it very well.

— *J. B. Priestley (*A Visit to New Zealand, *Heinemann, 1974)*

". . . I prefer amiable and cheerful dullards, not uncommon in New Zealand, to aggressive chip-on-the-shoulder types, not uncommon in Australia . . .

— *J. B. Priestley (*A Visit to New Zealand, *Heinemann, 1974)*

Charles Orwell Brasch (1909–1973) was born in Dunedin. A poet, editor and arts patron, Brasch was the founding editor of the literary journal *Landfall*, and through his 20 years of editing the journal, had a significant impact on the development of a literary and artistic culture in New Zealand. At the same time he provided substantial philanthropic support to the arts in New Zealand, including establishing a number of arts fellowships, providing financial support to New Zealand writers and artists during his lifetime, and bequeathing his extensive collection of books and artwork in his will to the Hocken Library and the University of Otago.

"

Both islands looked steep, many folded, the coasts of the sounds often sheer, and bare and scored. . . . Haze softened the air and turned the mountains blue. . . . The Kaikouras were distinct only in outline, streaks of snow marking Tapuaenuku. The hills of Wellington from the sea were as bare, yellow and dry as I remembered . . . The magnificence of the approach to the country set me soaring.

— *Charles Brasch* (Indirections: A Memoir 1909–1947,
Oxford University Press, 1980)

"

Basil Cairns Dowling (1910–2000) was a New Zealand, later British poet. Born in Southbridge, Canterbury, Dowling was educated in Christchurch at St Andrew's College then Canterbury University College. His first three collections of poems were published by Caxton Press, and he was regarded as a 'southern poet' and associated with Charles Brasch and Ruth Dallas. Many of his poems refer to his Christchurch youth and much of his poetry alludes to alienation both from a bucolic New Zealand childhood and from the English pastoral literary tradition.

> On this great plain the eye
> Sees less of land than sky . . .

— *Basil Dowling ('Canterbury',
Canterbury and Other Poems,
The Caxton Press, 1949)*

> We in these islands are
> Nowhere far from the sea . . .

— *Basil Dowling ('A Calm Day' from* Nowhere Far from the Sea: An Anthology
of New Zealand Poems for Secondary School Students, *Hogan, Helen M.
(compiler), Whitcombe & Tombs, 1971)*

James Keir Baxter (1926–1972) was a New Zealand poet and playwright, one of the country's most well-known and controversial literary figures and a prolific writer who produced numerous poems, plays and articles in his short life. He converted to Catholicism and established a controversial commune at Jerusalem, near Whanganui, in 1969. His bearded and shabby appearance, and outspoken attitudes towards the authorities, earned him a dubious national celebrity. He viewed middle-class society as a specious and hypocritical 'civilized coma', fenced off 'From the forces of revolt and lamentation' by the police. He was married to writer Jacquie Sturm.

"These unshaped islands, on the sawyer's bench, Wait for the chisel of the mind . . .

— *James K. Baxter ('New Zealand - for Monte Holcroft')*,
Collected Poems J. K. Baxter, *Oxford University Press, 1979)*

Maurice Francis Richard Shadbolt (1932–2004) was a New Zealand writer and occasional playwright. Born in Auckland, Shadbolt was educated at Te Kuiti High School, Avondale College and Auckland University College. In the 1960s, he moved to Titirangi with his family, buying a house that overlooked Little Muddy Creek where he spent the next 42 years writing. He won the Katherine Mansfield Memorial Award for a short story three times. Best known of his novels are *Strangers and Journeys* (1972), *The Lovelock Version* (1980), *Season of the Jew* (1986) and *Monday›s Warriors* (1990). A film version of his play *Once on Chunuk Bair* (1982) was released in 1991.

New Zealand begins with the sea and ends with the sea. Understand this and you begin to comprehend New Zealand and the New Zealander. The thundering surf is our frontier. And our only frontier guards, gulls and migratory birds. With justice, then, the Polynesian Voyagers called the land Tiritiri o te moana – the gift of the sea.

*— Maurice Shadbolt (*New Zealand Gift of the Sea, Whitcombe & Tombs, *1963)*

Gerald Malcolm Durrell, (1925–1995) was a British naturalist, writer, zookeeper, conservationist, and television presenter. He founded the Durrell Wildlife Conservation Trust and the Jersey Zoo on the Channel Island of Jersey in 1959. He wrote approximately 40 books, mainly about his life as an animal collector and enthusiast, the most famous being *My Family and Other Animals* (1956). Those memoirs of his family's years living in Greece were adapted into two television series (*My Family and Other Animals*, and *The Durrells*) and one television film (*My Family and Other Animals*, 2005). He was the youngest brother of novelist Lawrence Durrell.

"

I shall always attribute my uncertain start in New Zealand to the fact that I was introduced too early to what is known as the 'six o'clock swill'. In order to prevent people getting drunk the pubs close at six, just after the workers leave work. This means they have to leave their place of employment, rush frantically to the nearest pub, and make a desperate attempt to drink as much beer as they can in the shortest possible time. As a means of cutting down drunkenness, this is quite one of the most illogical deterrents I have come across.

— *Gerald Durrell, (*Two in the Bush*, Collins, 1966)*

"

Dame Edith Ngaio Marsh (1895–1982) was a New Zealand mystery writer and theatre director. Between 1913 and 1919 Marsh attended Canterbury College School of Art as a part-time student, supplementing her income with private tutoring. In 1928 she travelled to England and before returning to New Zealand she completed the draft of a detective novel, *A Man Lay Dead*, which was published in 1934, the first of numerous detective stories she would write. For much of the remainder of her life Ngaio Marsh divided her time between lengthy visits to England and her house in Cashmere, where she did her writing. She was appointed a Dame Commander of the Order of the British Empire in 1966.

"There, as abruptly as if one had looked over a wall, are the Plains, spread out beyond the limit of vision, laced with early mist, and a great river, bounded on the east by the Pacific, on the west by mere distance, and from east to west by a lordly sequence of mountains, rose-coloured where they received the rising sun.

— *Ngaio Marsh (describing the Canterbury Plains,* Black Beech and Honeydew, *Collins, 1965)*

Jim Henderson (1918-2005) was an author, broadcaster and historian. Born near Motueka he attended Nelson College then worked as a reporter on the *Nelson Evening Mail* and later on *The Free Lance*. During WWII Henderson served as a gunner with the 2nd NZ Expeditionary Force, losing a leg in a German attack. He was a prisoner of war in Italy for nearly two years. His hugely successful book *Gunner Inglorious* captured his wartime experiences. During the 1960s and 1970s his love of the country's rural life found expression in his popular radio programme, *Open Country* the material for which found its way into numerous books of the same name.

"Two days in Milford [Sound], that's quite enough, and you're put in your proper perspective . . .

— *Jim Henderson [and James Siers]*
(The New Zealanders, Millwood Press, 1975)

Michael King (1945–2004) was a New Zealand historian, author, and biographer. He wrote or edited over 30 books on New Zealand topics, including the best-selling *Penguin History of New Zealand*, which was the most popular New Zealand book of 2004. King was born in Wellington and grew up at Paremata. He studied history at Victoria University of Wellington, working part-time for the *Evening Post*. Later King worked full-time as a journalist at the *Waikato Times* newspaper covering Māori issues. After a number of years as a self-employed writer he returned to the University of Waikato in 1977 to complete a doctoral thesis on Te Puea Hērangi.

> In a country inhabited for a mere one thousand years, everybody is an immigrant or a descendant of immigrants.
>
> — *Michael King (Being Pakeha, Penguin, 1985)*

David James Bellamy (1933–2019) was an English botanist, television presenter, author and environmental campaigner. He published many scientific papers and books with many of the books associated with TV series on which he worked. When the New Zealand Tourism Department became involved with the Coast to Coast adventure race in 1988 they organised and funded foreign journalists to come and cover the event. One of those was Bellamy, who did not just report from the event, but decided to compete. While in the country, Bellamy worked on a documentary series, *Moa's Ark*, that was released by Television New Zealand in 1990.

"This is the greenest country in the world in more ways than one, shouting a message of hope to a dying world. I tell you, if New Zealand can't make it work, the rest of the world hasn't a chance.

— *David Bellamy*

Bryan Gould (1939–)

Bryan Charles Gould is a New Zealand-born British former politician and diplomat. Born in Hāwera, he studied at Victoria University College and Auckland University College before attending Balliol College, Oxford as a New Zealand Rhodes Scholar. After completing a degree in Law with first-class honours, he joined the British Diplomatic Service in 1964. He served as a Member of Parliament in Britain from 1974 to 1979, and again from 1983 to 1994. He was a member of the Labour Party's Shadow Cabinet from 1986 to 1992, and stood unsuccessfully for the leadership of the party in 1992. Gould returned to New Zealand in the 1990s, becoming Vice-Chancellor of the University of Waikato until his retirement in 2004.

"Everyone should have a New Zealand childhood.

— *Bryan Gould* (Goodbye to All That, *Macmillan, 1995*)

Lewis Niles Black (1948–) is an American stand-up comedian and actor. His comedy routines often escalate into angry rants about history, politics, religion, or any other cultural trends. He hosted the Comedy Central series *Lewis Black's Root of All Evil* and makesre gular appearances on *The Daily Show*.

Now, they say that New Zealand is beautiful and I do not know — because after 20 hours on a plane any landmass would be beautiful. I was just pleased there was anything there.

— *Lewis Black (reported in the* New Zealand Herald *13 May 2003)*

BIOGRAPHY SOURCES

PAGE 6: *Tasman*
Article uses material from the Wikipedia article https://en.wikipedia.org/wiki/Abel_Tasman
which is released under the Creative Commons — Attribution-ShareAlike 3.0 New Zealand — CC BY-SA 3.0 NZ

PAGE 8: *Parkinson*
Article uses material from the Wikipedia article https://en.wikipedia.org/wiki/Sydney_Parkinson which is released under the Creative Commons — Attribution-ShareAlike 3.0 New Zealand — CC BY-SA 3.0 NZ

PAGE 10: *Simonov*
Article uses material from the Wikipedia article https://en.wikipedia.org/wiki/Ivan_Mikhailovich_Simonov which is released under the Creative Commons — Attribution-ShareAlike 3.0 New Zealand — CC BY-SA 3.0 NZ

PAGE 12: *Thomson*
Article uses material from the Wikipedia article https://en.wikipedia.org/wiki/Arthur_Saunders_Thomson which is released under the Creative Commons — Attribution-ShareAlike 3.0 New Zealand — CC BY-SA 3.0 NZ

PAGE 14: *Courage*
Article uses material from the Wikipedia article Courage, Sarah Amelia, 1845?-1901 | Items | National Library of New Zealand | National Library of New Zealand (natlib.govt.nz)

PAGE 16: *Barker*
Article uses material from the Wikipedia article https://en.wikipedia.org/wiki/Mary_Anne_Barker which is released under the Creative Commons — Attribution-ShareAlike 3.0 New Zealand — CC BY-SA 3.0 NZ

PAGE 18: *Twain*
Article uses material from the Wikipedia article https://en.wikipedia.org/wiki/Mark_Twain which is released under the Creative Commons — Attribution-ShareAlike 3.0 New Zealand — CC BY-SA 3.0 NZ

PAGE 20: *Henry*
Article uses material from the Wikipedia article https://en.wikipedia.org/wiki/Richard_Henry_(conservationist) which is released under the Creative Commons — Attribution-ShareAlike 3.0 New Zealand — CC BY-SA 3.0 NZ

PAGE 22: *Reeves*
Article uses material from the Wikipedia article https://en.wikipedia.org/wiki/William_Pember_Reeves which is released under the Creative Commons — Attribution-ShareAlike 3.0 New Zealand — CC BY-SA 3.0 NZ

PAGE 24: *Blomfield*
Article uses material from the Wikipedia article https://en.wikipedia.org/wiki/Charles_Blomfield_(artist) which is released under the Creative Commons — Attribution-ShareAlike 3.0 New Zealand — CC BY-SA 3.0 NZ

PAGE 52: Baxter
Article uses material from the Wikipedia article https://en.wikipedia.org/wiki/James_K._Baxter which is released under the Creative Commons — Attribution-ShareAlike 3.0 New Zealand — CC BY-SA 3.0 NZ,. Also from 'James K Baxter', URL: https://nzhistory.govt.nz/people/james-k-baxter, (Ministry for Culture and Heritage), updated 8-Nov-2017

PAGE 54: Shadbolt
Article uses material from the Wikipedia article https://en.wikipedia.org/wiki/Maurice_Shadbolt which is released under the Creative Commons — Attribution-ShareAlike 3.0 New Zealand — CC BY-SA 3.0 NZ

PAGE 56: Durrell
Article uses material from the Wikipedia article https://en.wikipedia.org/wiki/Gerald_Durrell which is released under the Creative Commons — Attribution-ShareAlike 3.0 New Zealand — CC BY-SA 3.0 NZ

PAGE 58: Marsh
Article uses material from the Wikipedia article https://en.wikipedia.org/wiki/Ngaio_Marsh which is released under the Creative Commons — Attribution-ShareAlike 3.0 New Zealand — CC BY-SA 3.0 NZ. Also material from https://teara.govt.nz/en/biographies/4m42/marsh-edith-ngaio

PAGE 60: Henderson
Article uses material from various sources

PAGE 62: King
Article uses material from the Wikipedia article https://en.wikipedia.org/wiki/Michael_King_(historian) which is released under the Creative Commons — Attribution-ShareAlike 3.0 New Zealand — CC BY-SA 3.0 NZ

PAGE 64: Bellamy
Article uses material from the Wikipedia article https://en.wikipedia.org/wiki/David_Bellamy which is released under the Creative Commons — Attribution-ShareAlike 3.0 New Zealand — CC BY-SA 3.0 NZ

PAGE 66: Gould
Article uses material from the Wikipedia article https://en.wikipedia.org/wiki/Bryan_Gould which is released under the Creative Commons — Attribution-ShareAlike 3.0 New Zealand — CC BY-SA 3.0 NZ

PAGE 68: Black
Article uses material from the Wikipedia article https://en.wikipedia.org/wiki/Lewis_Black which is released under the Creative Commons — Attribution-ShareAlike 3.0 New Zealand — CC BY-SA 3.0 NZ